DELTA Business Communication Skills

Series editors
Susan Lowe and Louise Pile

Negotiating

Susan Lowe and Louise Pile

DELTA Publishing
Quince Cottage
Hoe Lane
Peaslake
Surrey GU5 9SW
England

www.deltapublishing.co.uk

© DELTA Publishing 2007

All rights reserved. No reproduction, copy or
transmission of this publication may be made
without written permission from the publishers
or in accordance with the provisions of the
Copyright, Designs and Patents Act 1988,
or under the terms of any licence permitting
copying issued by the Copyright Licensing
Agency, 90 Tottenham Court Road,
London W1P 9HE.

PHOTOCOPIABLE
Pages 46–53 may be photocopied for
use in class but may not be sold or
distributed separately or included in any
other publication for sale or distribution.

First published 2007
Reprinted 2009

Edited by Catriona Watson-Brown
Designed by Caroline Johnston
Cover design by Peter Bushell
Picture research by Emma Bree
Printed in Malta by Melita Press

Photo acknowledgments
Cover: Pictor/Imagestate; Real World People/Alamy
Page 8: Pictor/Imagestate/Alamy
Page 11: Business Cartoons
Page 14: The Copyright Group; Photolibrary
Page 20: Pictor/Imagestate/Alamy
Page 26: Real World People/Alamy
Page 27: L. Williams, M. Prince/Corbis
Page 30: S.S. Miric/Superstock
Page 34: J. Feingersh/Zefa/Corbis
Page 40: G. Baden/Corbis
Page 41: U. Kaiser/Corbis

ISBN 978-1-905085-13-2

Contents

Introduction	4
Needs analysis	5
Learning journal	6
Unit 1: Preparing to negotiate	8
Unit 2: Opening the negotiation	14
Unit 3: Making proposals	20
Unit 4: Reaching agreement	26
Unit 5: Involving others	34
Unit 6: Concluding the deal	40
Resources	46
Transcripts and answer keys	54

Introduction

DELTA Business Communication Skills is a new series which uses a learner-centred approach to develop key communication and language skills essential for today's international business environment. The series is designed for learners of business English at pre-intermediate and intermediate level, either pre-service or in-service, and it can be used either in the classroom or for self-study.

Features of the series include:

- Individual Needs analysis and Learning journal
- Awareness-raising activities
- Extensive personalized exercises
- Tips for effective performance in business
- Helpful suggestions for language study
- Regular language reference and review sections
- Photocopiable resources
- An integrated audio CD
- Full transcripts and answer keys

Negotiating aims to develop the skills and language needed to negotiate effectively in English, whether internally within an organization or externally with business partners; in a team or individually. *Negotiating* consists of six core units, each containing:

- **Context** – to raise awareness of the skills and issues (including cultural aspects) involved in the various activities of negotiating, and to introduce different strategies for developing these skills
- **Presentation** and **Practice** – of core language (vocabulary, functional phrases and pronunciation) linked to these skills
- **Tips** (cultural or language related) – on how to be more effective when negotiating
- **Consolidation** – to allow you to apply what you have learned to your own work situation.
- **Reference** – useful phrases and vocabulary related to each unit
- **Review** – study suggestions and further practice (ideal for homework/self-study)

The book also contains:

- **Needs analysis**. This encourages you to consider what you need to focus on in order to get the most out of the book and your learning.
- **Learning journal**. This provides the opportunity to reflect and personalize what you have studied in the book.
- **Resources section**. This provides additional material such as photocopiable frameworks and cards.
- **Answer key**. This is designed to enable you to work either alone or with a teacher.
- **Transcripts**. These detail the content of the accompanying CD.

How to use this book

Step 1

It is recommended that you start by working through the **Needs analysis** (page 5). This will help you to:

- think about your strengths and weaknesses in negotiating in English;
- identify and prioritize your immediate and future needs for negotiating;
- determine the order in which you work through the core units of this book.

Step 2

You should then familiarize yourself with the **Learning journal** (page 6), to which you are asked to refer at the end of every core unit.

Step 3

You should work through the units in the order they feel most appropriate to your needs and interests.

We hope you enjoy using this book.

Susan Lowe and Louise Pile
Authors

About the authors

Susan Lowe and Louise Pile have extensive general and Business English teaching and teacher training experience. They have written and edited a range of print and multimedia language-learning materials.

Needs analysis

1. a **Spend a few minutes thinking about what a negotiation is.**

   b **Now compare your ideas with the following definition.**

   > **negotiation** n. /nɪɡoʊʃˈeɪʃən/ a discussion between two or more people with different interests who are trying to reach agreement

2. **Negotiations can cover a wide range of business activities, from a formal discussion between a buyer and a supplier to agree terms, to an informal discussion with a colleague to confirm the next stages of a project.**

   a **Make a list of the different types of negotiation you have to take part in.**

   b **What do you find easy or challenging about negotiating in these situations?**

3. **Think about the following:**

   1 What skills and qualities do you think good negotiators need?
   2 What typical phases of a negotiation can you identify?
   3 What are the key elements of each phase?

   There are suggested answers on page 54.

4. **Each unit of this book focuses on a different area. Look through the unit summaries at the beginning of Units 1–6 and think about which areas you need to develop. Developing your awareness of what you already do well and what you could do better will allow you to focus on improving those skills you really need. Note down the units you intend to work through in order of priority for you – in terms of the area in which you feel you are weakest, or which is currently of most importance to you.**

Priority	Unit number and focus area
1	
2	
3	
4	
5	
6	

Before you start working through the units – starting with the one you listed as your top priority – look at the Learning journal on pages 6 and 7.

Learning journal

During the course As you work through each unit, summarize helpful language and tips for giving effective presentations from each unit. An example is given, but what you note down will depend upon your own learning pattern. You should also keep a note of areas that colleagues and friends have said you need to improve on.

Example

Unit: 3 **Useful language:** We are keen to … / An important consideration for us is … **Useful tips:** Use the present simple and/or present continuous when stating interests.	**Unit:** 4 **Useful language:** I propose that … / I propose + -ing **Useful tips:** Diplomatic language can soften a disagreement.

Your Learning journal

Unit: 1 **Useful language:** **Useful tips:**	**Unit:** 2 **Useful language:** **Useful tips:**
Unit: 3 **Useful language:** **Useful tips:**	**Unit:** 4 **Useful language:** **Useful tips:**
Unit: 5 **Useful language:** **Useful tips:**	**Unit:** 6 **Useful language:** **Useful tips:**

After the course It is important to consolidate your learning – both during your course and afterwards at work. After you have completed each unit, you should decide how you will continue to develop your skills, e.g. which consolidation/revision exercises you will do or how you will practise what you have learned in the workplace. Note that it is helpful to give yourself realistic deadlines!

Make notes on developing your skills, for example using a framework like the one below. An example is given to help you.

Example

> **Unit:** 3
>
> **Focus area:** Making proposals
>
> **I need to:**
> use more diplomatic language when rejecting a proposal.
>
> **To do this better, I intend to:**
> note down all the examples in Unit 3 and record myself saying them by 28 April. I will use two of the examples when I next reject a proposal.

Your planner

Unit:

Focus area:

I need to:

To do this better, I intend to:

This book is designed to be used during and after a course, so keep it with you and refer back to it whenever you need to, and keep adding to your notes!

Learning journal

UNIT 1

Preparing to negotiate

THIS UNIT LOOKS AT:
- the importance of preparing for a negotiation
- useful phrases for asking for, giving and responding to opinions
- useful phrases for prioritizing and giving reasons

Context

1 a **How important do you think preparing for a negotiation is? How do you / could you prepare for a negotiation?**

   b **Read this article extract about preparing for a negotiation. Do you agree with what Rupert Mack says? Give your reasons.**

> Good preparation is key to a successful negotiation, according to Rupert Mack, Head of Management Studies at Denton College.
>
> 'Being underprepared can mean you fail to reach agreement with the other party – that's why it's important to spend some time beforehand thinking about what you ideally want to get out of the negotiation, and what you are prepared to accept. Prioritize your aims – what's your main aim? What secondary goals do you have? Are you flexible about what you want to achieve? If you can't achieve your ideal goal, what would be an acceptable end to the negotiation for you – that is, the best alternative to a negotiated agreement (BATNA)?
>
> 'The next step is to consider the approach you will take – will you negotiate face to face or on the phone? Will you be on your own or as part of a team? What will your role be?
>
> 'Also try and find out as much as you can about the person or team you will be negotiating with – who are they? What's their role in the company? What might they want out of the negotiation? And what might their objections be to your proposals? If the other party is from a different culture, think how their way of negotiating might be the same as, or different from, your own. Consider how you might try to build trust and understanding, offer compromises and find common ground – crucial not just for the success of this negotiation but for building a long-term business relationship.
>
> 'It can be useful to run through your ideas with a colleague, ask their advice, and so on. If you are negotiating on behalf of others, perhaps a group of colleagues, take time to understand their concerns so that you can accurately represent their views.'

Tip See Unit 5 for more about working in teams and involving others in a negotiation.

2 🎧 **1.1 Listen to a negotiation between a designer and a retailer and answer these questions.**

1 How satisfactory was their preparation for the negotiation? Give your reasons.
2 How successfully do they negotiate the design fees? Give your reasons.

3 Think of the last negotiation you took part in.

- How successful were you in achieving your aim(s)?
- How did you prepare for the negotiation? How satisfactory was your preparation?

Presentation
Opinions

1 🎧 **1.2 Listen to two colleagues preparing to negotiate and answer these questions.**

1 What business do the speakers work in?
2 Who are they going to negotiate with?
3 What is their main aim?
4 What else do they hope to achieve in the negotiation?
5 What proposals do they consider making?
6 What objections might the other party have?
7 What offer do they decide to make?

Tip See Unit 3 for more about making and responding to proposals.

2 🎧 **1.2 Look at these phrases. Listen again and tick the phrases you hear.**

Asking for opinions
What do you think (about) ... ? ☐
What are your thoughts (on) ... ? ☐
How do you feel (about) ... ? ☐
What's your view/opinion (on) ... ? ☐
Do you think ... ? ☐
Do you agree? ☐

Giving opinions
I (don't) think we should / could / ought to ... ☐
You/We could (perhaps) ... ☐
It might be (a good idea to) ... ☐
Don't you think we should ... ? ☐
In my opinion/view, we should ... ☐

Responding to opinions
+
(That's a) good idea. ☐
That sounds good/fine (to me). ☐
I agree. ☐
–
I (can) see what you mean / your point, but ... ☐
I don't think (that would work). ☐
I'm not sure (I agree). ☐

Tip The infinitive without *to* is used after modal verbs (*should, might*, etc.), e.g. *It might work.*

Prioritizing and giving reasons

3 a Look at these sentences for prioritizing aims and giving reasons.

Prioritizing aims

- **I'd prefer to** focus on trying to reduce our working hours.
- Making a profit **is not as important as** building a long-term business relationship.

Giving reasons

- Cutting staff **would allow us to** remain profitable.
- Offering a discount **might enable us to** win the contract.

Tip See page 22 for more about disagreeing politely / in a diplomatic way.

Now look at the underlined phrases in the transcript on page 54. Which phrase(s) are used to:

1 prioritize aims
2 give reasons?

b Check your answers in the Reference section on page 12.

Pronunciation **4 a** Look at these verb/noun pairs, taken from the same transcript. Predict which syllable is stressed in each word.

1 object / objection
2 negotiate / negotiation
3 agree / agreement
4 prepare / preparation

b 🎧 1.3 Listen and mark the stressed syllable in each word.

Practice
Opinions

1 Match the sentence halves.

1 I can see
2 I think we should
3 How do you feel
4 That sounds
5 I'm not
6 I don't think

a about offering 10% off?
b good to me.
c what you mean.
d that would work.
e sure I agree.
f give a discount.

2 a Put these sentences into the correct order to reconstruct a dialogue between two American colleagues preparing to negotiate a contract.

a We could ask for $60 per hour for standard courses.

b That's a good idea, but what do you think we should do about our specialized programs?

c I think we should reduce our charges so that we're more competitive.

d I agree. We're far more expensive than other training companies. But what do you think we should charge?

e That sounds good to me. I'll let the rest of the team know our decisions.

f How do you feel about charging $100 – they do take longer to prepare?

b 🎧 1.4 Listen and check your answer.

1 Preparing to negotiate

Prioritizing and giving reasons

3 Complete these sentences appropriately.

1 I'd p_____ to hold the interviews next week rather than this week. This would e_____ us to have more time to prepare. I hope you have no objection.

2 The negotiation for the MFY contract isn't a_____ important for us as you might think b_____ it will only bring in $2,500.

3 It might be better to reduce our charges s_____ t_____ we remain competitive.

4 Our m_____ aim should be to maintain current staff numbers, a_____ we will not be able to cope with the workload otherwise.

5 I think we should ask for cheaper fittings. T_____ w_____ , we'll stay within our budget. Does anyone have any other proposals?

4 🎧 1.5 Listen to these words from the sentences in Exercise 3, and decide which syllable is stressed in each word.

1 prefer
2 enable
3 objection
4 negotiation
5 contract
6 competitive
7 maintain
8 workload
9 budget
10 proposals

5 Look at the transcript for audio 1.1 (page 54). What advice would you give each speaker for improving their negotiation skills?

Consolidation

1 Think of a negotiation you will soon be taking part in. Use the table on page 46 to help you prepare for the negotiation.

2 After the negotiation, take a few minutes to reflect on how successful the negotiation was. How satisfactory was your preparation?

→ NOW TURN TO YOUR LEARNING JOURNAL AND MAKE NOTES ON THIS UNIT.

Reference

Useful phrases

Asking for opinions

What do you think (about the offer)?

What are your thoughts (on their proposal)?

How do you feel (about the contract)?

What's your view/opinion (on the finances)?

Do you think we should (negotiate)?

Do you agree?

Giving opinions

I (don't) think we should / could / ought to (reduce the price).

You/We could (perhaps) agree to (offer a lower price).

It might be a good idea to (give a bonus).

Don't you think we should (question their figures)?

In my opinion/view, we should (find out more information).

Responding to opinions

+

(That's a) good idea.

That sounds good/fine (to me).

I agree.

−

I (can) see what you mean / your point, but (I'm not sure I agree).

I don't think that (would work).

I'm not sure (I agree).

Prioritizing

It would/might be better to (focus on getting an earlier delivery date).

I'd prefer to (negotiate over price) rather than (speed of delivery).

Our main aim should / ought to be to (get a competitive deal).

(Quantity) isn't as important as (quality).

(The delivery cost for Model 343) is less important than (for Model 958).

Giving reasons

because (of) / as

so that

This would/might mean that …

This means that …

This would allow/enable/help us to …

That way, we could …

Vocabulary

Contracts

to agree/agreement

to aim/aim

to budget/budget

to charge/charges

competitive

discount

fee

to fit/fittings

issue

to lower (a price)

to negotiate/negotiation/negotiator

objective

to prepare/preparation

to quote/quote

to reduce (a price)

satisfactory

to specify/specification

to succeed/success

Study suggestion Keep a record of typical mistakes, together with the correct version, for instance:
Incorrect: *I should to ask …*
Correct: *I should ask …*
Use this record as a checklist when reading through your written work.

Review

Skills 1 What tips would you give someone preparing for a negotiation?

2 🎧 1.6 Listen and decide what tips you would give Karen for preparing more effectively.

Useful phrases Some of these sentences contain errors. Find and correct them.

1 I don't think we should to sign the contract.
2 How do you feel about negotiate on your own?
3 I don't think that would work.
4 What your thoughts are on lowering the price?
5 It might be a good idea to consider their possible objections.
6 Our main aim ought be agreeing a realistic schedule.

Vocabulary Complete the table.

Verb	Noun
to specify	1 _____
2 _____	quote
to agree	3 _____
4 _____	fittings
to charge	5 _____
6 _____	negotiation

Pronunciation Choose five words from the vocabulary list of the Reference section. Mark the stressed syllable(s) in each word.

1 _____
2 _____
3 _____
4 _____
5 _____

1 Preparing to negotiate

UNIT 2

Opening the negotiation

THIS UNIT LOOKS AT:
- establishing rapport with negotiating partners and getting started
- useful phrases for making introductions and small talk
- useful phrases for setting the agenda and stating your interests

Context

1 **Match the elements of the opening phase of a negotiation (1–5) with their definitions (a–e).**

1 Welcome
2 Introductions
3 Small talk
4 Set the agenda
5 State interests

a This can break the ice and help non-native speakers get used to speaking English.
b This can make visitors feel that it is worth them having travelled.
c This is to clarify what everyone hopes to achieve from the negotiation.
d This is to outline how the negotiation will proceed.
e This is when everyone gets to know the others' names.

2 **Put the relevant number (1–6) on the line to show how often you do/would do each element when opening a negotiation.**

1 Welcome your business partner
2 Introduce yourself
3 Introduce your colleagues
4 Make small talk
5 Set the agenda
6 State your interests

| always | often | sometimes | rarely | never |

3 **Do you think someone from a different culture would put their numbers in the same places on the line?**

14 2 Opening the negotiation

Presentation
Opening the negotiation

1 🎧 **2.1** Listen to the beginning of a negotiation between two companies, Leclerc Electronics and By Design. By Design is a design agency with whom Leclerc Electronics is considering working. Decide if the following statements are true or false.

	True	False
1 The negotiation is taking place in the office of By Design.	☐	☐
2 Everyone knows one another already.	☐	☐
3 The two parties discuss the weather before starting business.	☐	☐
4 The two parties had outlined the general aims of the negotiation before the meeting.	☐	☐
5 Leclerc Electronics' interests are to find a cheap supplier.	☐	☐
6 By Design prefer working with business partners who give detailed information about what they want.	☐	☐

2 🎧 **2.1** Listen again and match the two parts of the phrases used in the negotiation.

1 Welcome to
2 My name is
3 I hope
4 Have you
5 Shall we get
6 I suggest we start
7 Leclerc Electronics is
8 An important consideration
9 We want
10 By Design is keen
11 We need to have a detailed

a a new image.
b been to Lyon before?
c brief.
d by clarifying what is needed.
e down to business?
f for us is to portray the correct image.
g Leclerc Electronics.
h looking to expand into new markets.
i Martin Stewart.
j to work with well-known companies.
k you had a good journey.

Tip Some cultures use first names early on in a negotiation, others prefer to use title and last name. To avoid overfamiliarity, use title and last name until you are invited to use first names.

3 a Put the phrases from Exercise 2 in the correct place in the table.

Welcoming	
Introducing yourself/colleagues	
Small talk	
Setting the agenda	
Stating interests	

Tip The present simple and present continuous can be used to state interests, e.g. *We want a new image; We are looking to expand into new markets.*

b Look at the transcript for audio 2.1 on page 56 and add more phrases to the table.

4 Match the informal phrases (1–7) with their equivalent formal phrases (a–g).

Informal	Formal
1 Welcome to …	a I suggest we begin by …
2 My name is …	b I hope you had a good journey.
3 Did you have a good journey?	c It is essential that we …
4 Is this your first trip to Dubai?	d Let me begin by welcoming you to …
5 How about starting with …?	e May I introduce myself, my name is …
6 We need to …	f This is your first trip to Dubai, I believe.
7 We want to …	g We are hoping to …

Pronunciation

5 a 🎧 **2.2 Listen to the pronunciation of the letter *o* in the word *to* in the following sentences. Does it sound long (/uː/ as in *too*) or short (/ə/ as in *tonight*)?**

	Long	Short
1 Welcome **to** Sanicare Installations.	☐	☐
2 I'd like **to** welcome you all this morning.	☐	☐
3 Are you looking forward **to** seeing the Eiffel Tower?	☐	☐
4 Our company is keen **to** work with upcoming companies.	☐	☐
5 We need **to** decide the schedules by the end of the week.	☐	☐
6 He's hoping **to** sign the contract as soon as possible.	☐	☐

b 🎧 **2.3 Now listen to the pronunciation of the letter *o* in the word *to* in bold in the following short dialogues.**

	Long	Short
1 Perhaps we don't need to discuss that now. No, I'm afraid we need **to**.	☐	☐
2 I'm not sure if you'd like to see some of the sights while you are here. Yes, I'd like **to**.	☐	☐
3 Monsieur Rivot hasn't really got time to get involved in this project. That's a shame, as he's very keen **to**.	☐	☐

Practice
Welcoming, introductions, small talk

1 a Complete these sentences.

1 Welcome _____ Brightside Datasystems.
2 May I introduce _____ , my name is Sarah Beecham.
3 _____ is my secretary, Tim Hunt.
4 Did you _____ a good journey?
5 Unfortunately, there was a _____ with the flight – we had to wait for two hours!
6 This is your first _____ to Dubai, I _____ .
7 I'm looking _____ to _____ some of the sights.

b 🎧 **2.4 Listen and check your answers.**

2 Opening the negotiation

Setting the agenda and stating interests

2 Put the words in order to make phrases for setting the agenda and stating interests.

1 business? / down / get / Shall / to / we
2 by / clarifying / I / situation. / start / suggest / the / we
3 are / expand / looking / into / markets. / new / to / We
4 An / consideration / customers. / existing / for / important / is / keep / to / us
5 aim / business / develop / in / the / to / USA. / We
6 are / high / keen / maintain / quality. / to / We

Present tenses

3 Correct these sentences. Focus on the verb tenses.

1 We are having a good reputation.
2 Our clients are needing to give us a detailed brief.
3 Maynard Plc currently looks to promote sales in Europe.
4 Our Head of Marketing launches a new campaign this month.
5 Is your Director wanting a decision today?
6 Do you look forward to visiting our city while you are here this week?

> **Tip** The present simple is used for states and facts. The present continuous is used for changing situations or things happening at the current time. Stative verbs (e.g. *want*, *need*) generally use the present simple.

Formal and informal

4 Write more informal phrases.

1 I'd like to introduce my colleague, Élodie Hussain.
2 I hope your hotel is comfortable.
3 May I suggest we begin by outlining the current situation.
4 We fully intend to launch our advertising campaign before the summer.
5 We are hopeful of a rise in sales by the end of the year.

Pronunciation

5 Practise saying the sentences and dialogues in Presentation Exercise 5. Pay particular attention to the pronunciation of the *o* in *to*.

Consolidation

1 Think of a negotiation you will take part in soon. Make some notes on the worksheet on page 47 to help you when opening the negotiation. Note phrases that you may use yourself or phrases you may hear your negotiating partner use.

2 Prepare what you will say to open the negotiation, expanding on the notes you made on the worksheet. Speak aloud.

3 After the negotiation, take a few moments to reflect on it:
- How did the opening stage go?
- What would you do differently next time? Why / Why not?

➜ NOW TURN TO YOUR LEARNING JOURNAL AND MAKE NOTES ON THIS UNIT.

Reference

Useful phrases

Welcoming
Welcome to ...
I'd like to welcome you to ...

Making introductions
My name is ...
This is ...
These are ...

Making small talk
I hope you had a good journey.
Have you been to ... before?
I hope to see some of the sights.
Is this your first trip to ...

Setting the agenda
Shall we get down to business?
I suggest we start by (looking at) ...

Stating interests
... is looking to ...
An important consideration for us is to ...
We want ...
... is keen to ...
We need to have ...

Vocabulary

Increasing business
contact person
detailed brief
to expand into new markets
Head of Sales
image
to launch a new campaign
to open up
to promote sales
to be recognized internationally
rise in sales
to sign a contract
solid client base
top-quality service
upcoming company
well-known company

Small talk
to be famous for
to look forward to (doing)
to see the sights
slight delay

Study suggestion Record yourself saying phrases and vocabulary you are likely to use in your own negotiation. Keep recording until you are happy with the way they sound. Listen to your recording when preparing for a negotiation to remind yourself.

Review

Skills Why do people spend some time at the beginning of a negotiation making small talk?
What else generally happens when opening a negotiation?

Useful phrases **1** Which phrases could you use in the following situations?

1 Welcoming your business partners to the negotiation.
2 Giving your name and your colleagues' names.
3 Setting the agenda.
4 Stating your interests.

2 Choose the correct form of the verb in the following sentences.

1 I *am hoping / hope* you had a good journey.
2 Our competitors *are having / have* more experience than us.
3 Our director *is holding / holds* negotiations at this very moment.
4 *Are you visiting / Do you visit* the factory as well as the research centre while you are here this week?

Vocabulary Complete the mind map with vocabulary relating to increasing business.

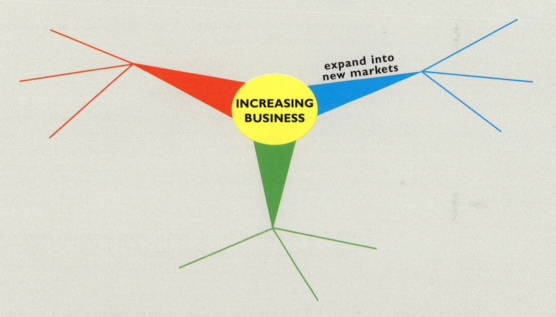

Pronunciation Say the phrases you noted in Exercise 1 of the Useful phrases section above. Pay attention to your pronunciation of the letter o in the word to. Should it be a long or short sound? Record yourself so that you can check your pronunciation.

UNIT 3

Making proposals

THIS UNIT LOOKS AT:
- making and responding to proposals
- useful phrases for making offers, reacting and making counter proposals
- ways of making language more diplomatic

Context

1 Read the extract below from a book on negotiating and answer these questions.

1 In a negotiation, when someone doesn't agree with a suggestion and they put an alternative forward instead, what is it called?

2 What sort of language can soften a negative reaction?

> At the proposal stage of a negotiation, delegates make proposals, react to them, and if they don't agree with the suggestion made, they may offer a counter-proposal as an alternative. When reacting to proposals, using diplomatic language such as 'I'm afraid that's not really what we had in mind' instead of 'No, that's not good enough' can help you sound less direct or negative. This can promote a good working relationship between you and your business partner, and is more likely to lead to a successful outcome in the negotiation.

2 What do you think? Do you find making proposals more difficult than responding to proposals? Why (not)?

Presentation
Making and responding to proposals

1 a 🎧 3.1 Listen to a negotiation between a departmental boss and his staff. Which grouping of teams represents the boss's original proposal?

20   3 Making proposals

b Which grouping represents the final decision?

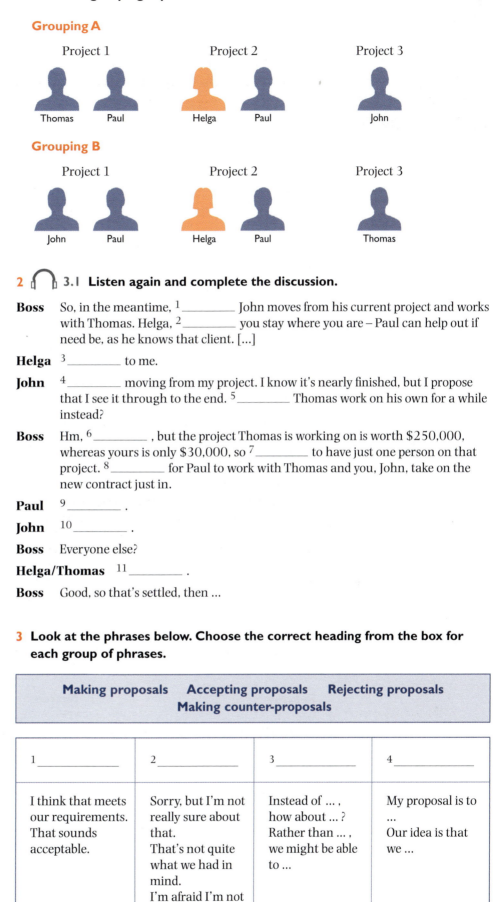

2 3.1 Listen again and complete the discussion.

Boss So, in the meantime, ¹_____ John moves from his current project and works with Thomas. Helga, ²_____ you stay where you are – Paul can help out if need be, as he knows that client. [...]

Helga ³_____ to me.

John ⁴_____ moving from my project. I know it's nearly finished, but I propose that I see it through to the end. ⁵_____ Thomas work on his own for a while instead?

Boss Hm, ⁶_____ , but the project Thomas is working on is worth $250,000, whereas yours is only $30,000, so ⁷_____ to have just one person on that project. ⁸_____ for Paul to work with Thomas and you, John, take on the new contract just in.

Paul ⁹_____ .

John ¹⁰_____ .

Boss Everyone else?

Helga/Thomas ¹¹_____ .

Boss Good, so that's settled, then ...

3 Look at the phrases below. Choose the correct heading from the box for each group of phrases.

| Making proposals   Accepting proposals   Rejecting proposals |
| Making counter-proposals |

1_____	2_____	3_____	4_____
I think that meets our requirements. That sounds acceptable.	Sorry, but I'm not really sure about that. That's not quite what we had in mind. I'm afraid I'm not convinced by that.	Instead of ... , how about ... ? Rather than ... , we might be able to ...	My proposal is to ... Our idea is that we ...

3 Making proposals

Diplomatic language

4 Find phrases in the transcript for audio 3.1 (page 58) that mean the same as these sentences.

1 It's a bad idea for me to move from my project.
2 I know you don't like that.
3 It's impossible having just one person on that project.

> **Tip** Diplomatic language uses *not* + positive word rather than the negative word of the same meaning, and it uses *I'm afraid* or *I'm sorry* to start a sentence.

5 Match the direct phrases (1–4) with their more diplomatic equivalents (a–d).

1 That's totally unacceptable
2 I cannot agree to that.
3 That is impossible!
4 That's a stupid idea!

a I'm afraid I can't really agree to that.
b I'm not sure that idea is realistic.
c I don't think we can accept that.
d I'm sorry, but that's not really a possibility.

6 Complete these sentences with the phrases in the box.

moving   propose   suggest that   we stay

1 I'd like to propose that _____ in this team.
2 We _____ you move to another department.
3 I'd like to _____ staying in this team.
4 We suggest _____ to another department.

Pronunciation

7 🎧 3.2 Listen and match the phrases (1–5) with the correct stress patterns (a–e).

1 I propose that you stay in this team.
2 We suggest postponing the project.
3 I can't agree to that, I'm afraid.
4 Could we delay the start date instead?
5 Yes, we can accept those conditions.

a ••●••●••●
b •●••●••●•••
c ●•••●••●•
d ••●•●•••●•
e ●•••●••●●•●

> **Tip** Notice the form of the verbs:
> *propose/suggest* + *that* + (verb phrase);
> *propose/suggest* + (-ing).

Practice
Making and responding to proposals

1 🎧 3.3 Listen and respond to the proposals. Use the prompts below telling you whether to accept, offer a counter-proposal or reject the offer.

Reaction	Reason
1 Accept	Owen has experience.
2 Reject	Cause too much disruption.
3 Reject Offer counter-proposal	Didn't work last time. Promote one of team members as development opportunity.
4 Accept	They work well together.

2 Complete these sentences with suitable expressions.

1 I'd like to propose that ...
2 My colleagues and I suggest ...
3 We propose ...
4 Having considered your proposals, my boss suggests ...
5 Last time we met, we proposed that ...

Diplomatic language

3 Make these sentences more diplomatic.

1 That's out of the question.
2 I can't accept that.
3 That's not good enough!
4 That's far too expensive.
5 Your delivery times are extremely slow.

Pronunciation

4 a Mark the stress on these sentences.

1 We suggest starting again.
2 I propose forming a new team.
3 We suggest asking our customers what they want.
4 I propose that we do some research first.
5 I'm afraid that's not really acceptable.
6 How about using a new supplier?
7 That's a good idea!

Tip Although there are fixed patterns of sentence stress, they can change according to context and individual speaking styles.

b **3.4 Say the sentences aloud, then listen to check your pronunciation.**

Consolidation

1 Think of a negotiation you will take part in soon. Note some possible proposals that you might use yourself or hear your counterpart use. Make notes on the worksheet on page 48.

2 Prepare what you will say to make and respond to the proposals, expanding on the notes you made on the worksheet. Speak aloud.

3 After the negotiation, take a few moments to reflect on it:

- Did you make your proposals effectively and did you respond well?
- Did you use diplomatic language?
- What would you do differently next time? Why / Why not?

 NOW TURN TO YOUR LEARNING JOURNAL AND MAKE NOTES ON THIS UNIT.

Reference

Useful phrases

Making proposals

My proposal is to …

Our idea is that we …

I'd like to propose that …

My suggestion is …

Accepting proposals

I think that meets our requirements.

That sounds acceptable.

That sounds reasonable.

I can accept that.

Fine.

Rejecting proposals

Sorry, but I'm not really sure about that.

That's not quite what we had in mind.

I'm afraid I'm not convinced by that.

I'm afraid I have some reservations about that.

Offering counter-proposals

Instead of … , how about … ?

Rather than … , we might be able to …

Could … instead?

Perhaps a better idea would be to …

Vocabulary

Team organization

to agree

client

contract

counter-proposal

customer

to delay the start date

to do research

to move from one project to another

to postpone a project

project

project leader

project management

proposal

to reorganize the team

to see a project through

to take a contract on

team

to work with someone

Study suggestion   Use cards to note useful phrases and possibly take them into the negotiation with you to help you to remember. You could use different-colour cards for different functions, or for more diplomatic phrases. You can also mark the word stress on the phrases.

Review

Skills Complete this paragraph about making proposals with suitable words.

If you don't agree with your business partner's proposal, you can ¹r_____ it and offer a ²c_____-p_____ , but it could be advisable to be ³d_____ in so doing. Your business partner might then ⁴a_____ your proposal.

Useful phrases 1 Write suitable phrases under the correct heading. Try to use diplomatic language where appropriate.

Making proposals	Accepting	Rejecting	Making counter proposals

2 Write the correct form of the verb in brackets.

1 We propose that _____ (outsource) the project will reduce costs.
2 I'd like to suggest _____ (delay) the start of the project.
3 I propose _____ (change) the team leader.
4 We suggest _____ (reorganize) the team.

Vocabulary Can you guess the words from their definitions?

1 To move the date when a project begins to a later date
2 A person who organizes a project team and takes control
3 To complete a project
4 To change the members of a team or their roles within it
5 To put forward a suggestion
6 To put forward an alternative suggestion

Pronunciation 🎧 3.4 Listen again to audio 3.4 and repeat the sentences, paying attention to the stress patterns.

UNIT 4

Reaching agreement

THIS UNIT LOOKS AT:
- **persuading and bargaining**
- **listening skills**
- **useful phrases for checking and clarifying, and giving reassurance**

Context 🎧 **4.1 Listen to an experienced negotiator speak about reaching agreement. Make notes on what he says about influencing people under the headings given.**

- persuading

- listening

- checking and clarifying

- giving reassurance

26 4 Reaching agreement

Presentation
Reaching agreement

1 Read the e-mail below from the Head of Communications to the management of Imagewise, a large PR agency, concerning the proposed move to new offices. Which of the following are mentioned?

1. Need a quiet working environment ☐
2. Need catering facilities ☐
3. Need new computing equipment ☐
4. Need a lot of storage space ☐
5. Need additional lighting ☐

From: Tita Aiguillar, Head of Communications
To: Terry Norton, Head of Estates
Date: 23 November
Subj.: Office move

Following the announcement to move the Communications Team to new open-plan offices, I would like to raise the following requests on behalf of our members.
I know you'll agree that our productivity relies on being able to work in a quiet environment. Also, I'm sure you'll appreciate that we require plenty of storage space. Our members are used to working in small, individual offices, and many have collected a great deal of paperwork over time.
If you can guarantee that quiet rooms will be made available for our members to use as and when they want, then we will accept the proposal for open-plan office space. Also, provided that additional storage is made available at the end of the floor for the team as a whole, then we could accept having a smaller cupboard by each desk, as proposed.
Regards
Tita

2 🎧 4.2 Listen to part of a negotiation between Tita Aiguillar and Terry Norton, who is overseeing the move to open-plan offices at Imagewise. Put the words in the box into the gaps to complete a summary of the negotiation.

> almost every day   avoid disturbing colleagues
> phone lines and Internet access   the archive

Tita asks for ¹_____ in all rooms. This means members of staff can ²_____ . She also asks for an area for ³_____ . Employees need access to it ⁴_____ .

Tip Skills and phrases used in internal negotiations can also be used in external ones.

3 🎧 **4.2 Read the e-mail on page 27 and listen to the negotiation again. Complete these phrases.**

Bargaining

1 If you _____ quiet rooms will be made available, then we will _____ for open-plan office space.
2 _____ additional storage is made available, _____ accept having a smaller cupboard.
3 _____ put in phone lines and Internet access to all rooms, _____ use any as a meeting room.
4 _____ provide additional storage somewhere on the floor, then _____ to manage with a small cupboard.

Persuading

5 I know _____ our productivity relies on being able to work in a quiet environment.
6 I'm sure _____ we require plenty of storage space.

Giving reassurance

7 I can _____ the number of rooms required is no different to the agreed plans.
8 You _____ your department has the standard amount of storage.

Tip Note the use of the conditionals when bargaining. The first conditional suggests there is a more real possibility, the second conditional suggests the outcome is less likely. (See page 61 for forming conditionals.)

4 Match the sentence halves.

1 If small desks are provided,
2 If the width of the aisle were reduced,
3 Members of staff located on the ground floor will be disadvantaged
4 Provided that overhead lighting is sufficient in the corner,
5 Disabled members of staff and visitors would have easy access throughout the building

a if lifts and ramps were provided.
b we could use the it as a hot-desk area.
c we will need extra surfaces for laying out our designs.
d it would be a fire hazard.
e if all the meeting rooms are located on the first floor only.

Tip It is advisable to give the condition before the offer because your counterpart will have to wait to hear what you have to say rather than interrupting.

Listening skills

5 🎧 **4.3 Listen again to the second part of the negotiation between Tita, Head of Communications, and Terry, Head of Estates. Are these statements true or false?**

	True	False
1 Terry agrees to give the Communications Team more storage.	☐	☐
2 Terry gives a clear *yes–no* answer.	☐	☐

Tip Learn to 'read between the lines': *I might meet Friday's deadline* does not necessarily mean *I will meet Friday's deadline*.

28 4 Reaching agreement

Pronunciation 6 🎧 **4.4 Listen to the following extract from the negotiation. Mark where it sounds as though the words run together.**

I mean, we could use the room for a meeting – perhaps for a teleconference – or equally, a member of staff may need to phone a colleague abroad, which will take a long time, so they could use the telephone in the room instead of at their desk, to avoid disturbing their colleagues.

Tip When speaking, native speakers often run sounds and words together.

Checking and clarifying 7 **Read the transcript of the negotiation (audio 4.2 on page 59). Underline the phrases used for clarifying and checking. These can be used to check you have understood properly.**

Practice 1 **Put this e-mail into the correct order.**

a   am sure you understand that our research scientists need a quiet and clean environment

b   I am writing with reference to the construction of the new research laboratory. I

c   If you can guarantee that dust will be dampened and that noise will be kept to a minimum,

d   in which to work. While we are looking forward to moving into new laboratories,

e   then we will be able to continue our work. If you cannot guarantee this,

f   we need reassurance from you that the building works will cause as little disruption as possible.

g   we will have to reconsider the works schedule.

Bargaining 2 **Complete the negotiation extracts below using these phrases.**

> can   If you   If you can guarantee that   provided
> then we will accept the proposal   we could

We need to be able to rely on our suppliers. ¹_____ shipping the computer hard drives from your factory in Eastern Europe is not going to delay the opening of our new office, ²_____ .

We need to be sure of high quality. ³_____ that you can supply reliable computer components, ⁴_____ consider placing an order with you.

⁵_____ include a two-year warranty for each item, we ⁶_____ sign the contract.

4 Reaching agreement

3 Complete the sentences below with the verbs from the box.

can start	continue	moved	shared	will become	would use

1 If we _____ from an open-plan area to individual offices, we would need more floor space, which would be too expensive.

2 If management _____ our open-plan area, they would realize how noisy and consequently unproductive it can be.

3 If the packing crates are delivered next week, we _____ emptying our cupboards for the move the following week.

4 Staff _____ restless if the office move is postponed again. They were frustrated by the initial delay.

5 More people _____ public transport when travelling to and from work if bus stops were located nearby.

6 If a hot-desk area is provided, staff can _____ to work while their computers are set up at their new desks.

Persuading and giving reassurance

4 Look at the cards at the top of page 49. Respond to each of the situations on them.

Listening skills

5 4.5 **Listen to these statements. What does the speaker *really* mean?**

1 a Dust and noise will definitely be minimized. ☐
  b Dust and noise might be minimized. ☐

2 a Research work definitely won't be delayed. ☐
  b Research work hopefully won't be delayed. ☐

3 a Staff will definitely have the amount of storage space they need. ☐
  b Staff should have the amount of storage space they need. ☐

6 a Read these sentences aloud, running words and sounds together as you think a native speaker might.

1 I am not sure if I have understood you correctly.
2 Would it be correct to say that you do not need teleconferencing facilities in all the meeting rooms?
3 Provided you can guarantee high-quality goods, I will accept your offer.

b 🎧 4.6 Listen and check your answers.

Checking and clarifying

7 a Look at the cards at the bottom of page 49. Put the phrases under the correct heading cards.

b Practise saying them.

c 🎧 4.7 Listen and use the phrases from the cards to clarify and respond.

Consolidation

1 Think of a negotiation you will take part in soon. Make some notes on the worksheet on page 50 to help you when reaching agreement.

2 Practise what you will say in the negotiation, using the notes you made on the worksheet. Speak aloud. Take care of and sounds/words that could run together. Record yourself.

3 After the negotiation, take a few moments to reflect on it:
- Did you reach agreement? Why? / Why not? How did it go?
- What would you do differently next time? Why? / Why not?

➔ NOW TURN TO YOUR LEARNING JOURNAL AND MAKE NOTES ON THIS UNIT.

Reference

Useful phrases

Bargaining

If you can guarantee that ... , then we will accept the proposal.

Provided that ... , then we could accept ...

If you ... , we could ...

If you can ... , then we are prepared to ...

Persuading

I know you'll agree that ...

I'm sure you'll agree that ...

Giving reassurance

I can assure you that ...

You can be sure that ...

Checking you've understood correctly

I'm sorry, did you say ... ?

When you said ... , did you mean ... ?

I'm sorry, I didn't catch that.

I'm not sure if I've understood you correctly.

Showing understanding

Yes, I see.

Right.

OK.

A-ha, yes.

Clarifying

No, not exactly.

That's not really what I meant.

What I wanted to say was ...

Vocabulary

Office relocation

aisle

clean environment

construction work

desk

disruption

dust

hot-desk area

individual office

meeting room

to move

noise

office space

overhead lighting

phone line

plans

quiet room

research laboratory

storage space

surface

Study suggestion Watch English films with subtitles and listen to the way in which native speakers run sounds and words together. Try to imitate them.

Review

Skills Write some tips for reaching agreement. Use the following headings: persuading, listening, checking and clarifying, giving reassurance.

Useful phrases

1 Unjumble these phrases.

1 correctly. / if / I'm / I've / not / sure / understood / you
2 agree to / disturbance / is / minimal, / next month. / Provided / starting / that / the work / we
3 agree / I / know / that ... / you'll
4 assure / can / I / that ... / you

2 Write the correct form of the verb in brackets to complete these sentences.

1 If you can guarantee quick delivery, we _____ (order) 20,000 units.
2 If building work started next month, production _____ (be delayed) and we might lose the contract.
3 New lighting _____ (be installed) if the existing lighting didn't meet Health and Safety requirements.
4 Productivity _____ (drop) in summer if we don't have air conditioning.

Vocabulary Complete the crossword with vocabulary relating to negotiating an office move.

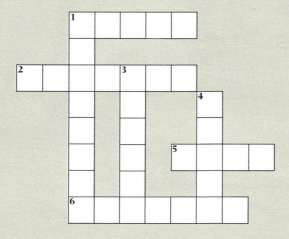

Across

1 the intended layout of an office
2 cupboard space
5 place where meetings can be held
6 to cause disruption

Down

1 _____ that you deliver on time, we can accept.
3 Disabled staff need easy _____ to their desks.
4 a level in an office building

Pronunciation 🎧 4.3 Mark on the transcript for audio 4.3 (page 59) the sounds and words that you think run together. Then listen again to audio 4.3 and check your answer.

UNIT 5

Involving others

THIS UNIT LOOKS AT:
- working as part of a negotiating team
- useful phrases for taking turns and keeping people informed
- useful phrases for asking and answering questions, and making spontaneous decisions

Context

Make notes on these questions.

1 What is your experience of negotiating as part of a team?
2 What are the advantages of negotiating in a team? Are there any disadvantages?
3 What do you think makes an effective negotiating team?
4 In what situations might it be useful to involve other people in a negotiation? At what stage of the negotiation?

Presentation

1 5.1 You will hear members of the Communications Department at Logitel, an international logistics company, having a teleconference. Listen and decide if these statements are true or false.

Tip During a teleconference, it can be helpful to address other people by name to avoid confusion.

1 Three people are taking part in the negotiation.
2 Anna is leading the negotiation.
3 The London team will manage the production of the annual report this year.

L·O·G·I·T·E·L

34   5 Involving others

Taking turns 2 🎧 **5.1 Read these phrases for involving others in the negotiation. Listen again and tick those you hear the speakers use.**

1 … , what do you think? ☐
2 Let's ask … (about that). ☐
3 Would you like to ask anything else? ☐
4 I'll have to check with … ☐
5 Perhaps you could answer that, … ☐
6 I'd now like to ask … to speak (about that). ☐
7 … , do you have anything to add? ☐
8 … , could you say something (about that)? ☐
9 I'm sure you'll all agree. ☐
10 As I'm sure you all know, … ☐

Questions and answers 3 **a To get information from the other people you are negotiating with, you can ask open questions such as those below (1–4). For each one, give the function (a–d) of the answer.**

> **Tip** Open questions usually start *How much, How, What, When, Who, Where,* etc.

a delaying/avoiding giving a direct answer
b giving a vague answer
c reacting positively to a negative question
d referring a question to someone else

1 Q But why should we do that?
   A I'm glad you asked that. [c]
2 Q How much is each container?
   A Around €500, I'd say. ☐
3 Q Can you tell us more about your relocation plans?
   A I'm afraid I'd have to ask Bill. ☐
4 Q Could you say exactly how much that would cost?
   A I'd like to come to that later. ☐

> **Tip** To avoid asking questions that appear too direct/rude, you can say *Can/Could you tell me … ?*

b Look through the transcript for audio 5.1 (page 61) and find examples of open questions to complete these prompts.

1 What's the … ?
2 Could you tell us … ?
3 Who needs … ?

Pronunciation 4 🎧 **5.2 Listen to the way the speaker's voice rises and falls in each of these questions. Now practise asking the questions, making your voice rise and fall in the same way.**

Spontaneous decisions

5 **Look at these phrases for making spontaneous decisions. Now find examples of spontaneous decisions in the transcript for audio 5.1 (page 61).**

- I'm really tired. **I think I'll** take a break.
- I can't do this on my own. **I'll** have to call my boss for some advice.
- I've made a decision. **I'm going to** book the appointment now.
- We've almost finished. **I think I'm going to** go home a bit earlier tonight.

Keeping people informed

6 **Rearrange the words to find phrases to keep people informed. Which of them are used in audio 5.1?**

1 a / down. / I / Just / minute / note / that / while
2 bear / find / happened. / I / me / out / Please / what's / while / with
3 a / e-mail. / Excuse / I / me / quick / send / while

Practice

Taking turns and keeping people informed

1 **All but one of these phrases contain errors. Find and correct them.**

1 Perhaps you could to answer that question, Sandra?
2 Let ask Alexis about the plans.
3 I will have to check with my boss.
4 Could you saying something about the planning stage, Siobhan?
5 I'm sure you'll all be agree that it's a good idea.
6 Please bear me while I make a quick phone call.
7 Just a minute I consult a colleague.
8 Would you like ask anything else?

Questions and answers

2 a What would you say in response to these questions? Follow the prompts.

1 What is the deadline for getting the delivery to you?
   (Give vague answer.)
2 So, why should I place an order with you and not another stationery company?
   (You are nervous and can't think what to say. Refer to someone else.)
3 Why are you just offering us just 10 per cent off? As a valued customer, we expect a lot more than that.
   (React positively.)
4 Could you tell me when you will be making a decision?
   (Avoid giving a direct answer.)

b **5.3 Listen to some example answers.**

Spontaneous decisions

3 Make some spontaneous decisions in response to these prompts.

1 I really need some help setting up this database.
2 Is anyone going near the station after our negotiation? I need to get there by 5.30 at the latest.
3 We could really do with advice from someone from the senior management team.
4 You don't look very well – are you sure you still want to take part in the negotiation?

4 In preparation for your next negotiation, make a list of questions that the other party could ask you. Then practise answering these questions.

Question	Answer

Consolidation

1 Think of a negotiation you have recently taken part in.

- Did you negotiate alone? as part of a team?
- What was your role?

2 Think of a negotiation you are going to take part in. Use the checklist on page 51 to help you prepare.

3 After the negotiation, take a few minutes to reflect on it – what went well, what didn't go so well and so on.

➡ NOW TURN TO YOUR LEARNING JOURNAL AND MAKE NOTES ON THIS UNIT.

Reference

Useful phrases

Taking turns

… , what do you think?

Let's ask … (about that).

… , would you like to say something?

I'll have to check with …

… , perhaps you could answer that.

I'd now like to ask … to speak (about that).

… , do you have anything to add?

… , could you say something (about that).

I'm sure you'll all agree …

As I'm sure you all know, …

Making decisions

(I think) I'll / I will …

(I think) I'm going to / I am going to …

Asking and answering questions

Can you tell me / say … ?

Could you tell me / say … ?

That's an interesting question / a good point.

I'm afraid I'll have to ask …

Around/About (€345), I'd say.

That depends.

I'd like to come to / talk about that later.

Keeping people informed

Just a minute while I note that down.

Please bear with me while I find out what's happened.

Excuse me while I send a quick e-mail.

Vocabulary

Projects

to agree (schedules)

to brief someone

CEO

to confirm a deadline

(to deliver) a consignment

deadline

(to make) a deal

to draw up (a list)

effective

expertise

to make notes

to monitor discussions

to note down

one-off (event)

outcomes

(joint) project

to sign a contract

skills

to take the lead

Study suggestion Ask a colleague to ask you the questions you wrote down in Consolidation and practise giving the answers. Record yourself. Afterwards, think about how confident you sounded, how fluent, etc.

Review

Skills Do you agree or disagree with these statements? Give your reasons.

1 It's always better to negotiate face to face than on the phone, etc.
2 It's always better to negotiate one to one than in a team.

Useful phrases Note down some useful phrases under these headings. Then check your answers in the Reference section.

Taking turns	Making decisions	Keeping people informed

Vocabulary Match the pairs as they are used in the unit. Then check your answers in the Reference section.

1 to make   a schedules
2 to sign   b a deal
3 to agree   c a list
4 to take   d a contract
5 to brief   e someone
6 to draw up   f the lead

Pronunciation Write six open questions you could use in a negotiation. Practise saying these aloud, paying attention to how your voice rises; perhaps record yourself.

1 How …
2 When …
3 Where …
4 Can you tell me …
5 Could you tell me …
6 Who …

UNIT 6

Concluding the deal

THIS UNIT LOOKS AT:
- ending a negotiation effectively
- useful phrases for summarizing and confirming agreement
- useful phrases for outlining future action and thanking/saying goodbye

Context

1 **Think of a recent negotiation you have (or someone you know has) been involved in.**

- What was the outcome of the negotiation?
- Were all the key points covered during the negotiation?
- Did you agree to discuss any other issues at a later date?
- Did one of the parties summarize what was agreed (e.g. at the end of the negotiation or in a written follow-up)?
- Were there any misunderstandings? If so, were these related to language? cultural differences? different assumptions/agendas? communication styles?
- What future action(s) did each party agree to do following the negotiation?

Tip A written summary can be a useful record of all the points discussed.

2 **Look these tips for ending a negotiation effectively. Do you agree with the advice? What other advice would you give?**

- Summarize all the points that you have discussed.
- Confirm what has been agreed.
- Outline future actions – who will do what, by when, etc.
- Thank everyone for taking part and say goodbye.

Tip End the negotiation on a positive note by engaging in small talk.

6 Concluding the deal

Presentation

1 🎧 6.1 **Emily Schmidt, a conference organizer, is coming to the end of her negotiation with a soft-drinks supplier. Listen and decide if these statements are true or false.**

	True	False
1 Emily has ordered over 400 bottles of mineral water.	☐	☐
2 The supplier will deliver the order to the conference venue.	☐	☐
3 Emily will pay the supplier by the end of the month.	☐	☐
4 Emily and the supplier still need to discuss the details of the delivery.	☐	☐

Concluding a negotiation

2 🎧 6.1 **Here are some useful phrases for concluding a negotiation. Listen again and tick which phrase in each pair is used.**

1 a Perhaps I could just summarize what we've agreed?   ☐
  b Can I just go over what we've agreed?   ☐
2 a Do you have anything to add?   ☐
  b Have I missed anything out?   ☐
3 a One point we need to agree is a suitable delivery time.   ☐
  b As agreed, we will contact you about a suitable delivery time.   ☐
4 a I look forward to speaking to you again then. Bye.   ☐
  b Thank you – and goodbye.   ☐

3 a **Put the phrases from Exercise 2 in the correct place in the table.**

Summarizing	Confirming agreement / Responding	Outlining future action	Thanking/ Saying goodbye

b **Put the cards on page 52 into pairs to find more phrases. Add these to the table above.**

Tip You can use *will* and *going to* to outline future action, e.g. *As agreed, you will send a written summary.*

6 Concluding the deal

Pronunciation

4 🎧 **6.2** Listen to some of the sentences from audio 6.1. Mark the word(s) that are stressed in each sentence.

1 You're going to supply us with 100 bottles of still and 200 bottles of sparkling water.
2 The total cost to us will be €456.
3 We have agreed to pay in full within 25 working days.

Practice
Concluding a negotiation

1 a Match the sentence halves.

1 Are you happy   a agree?
2 Do we need to   b anything to add?
3 Do you have   c discuss anything else?
4 Do you   d missed anything out?
5 Have I   e with that?

b Look at the phrases for responding in the Reference section (page 44). Practise saying them to respond to the questions above.

c 🎧 **6.3** Listen to some examples.

2 Put the words into the correct order to make useful phrases for concluding a negotiation.

1 agreed. / could / I / just / Perhaps / summarize / we've / what
2 everything. / for / Thank / you
3 anything / discuss / Do / else? / need / to / we
4 a / agreed, / As / send / summary. / We / will / written / you
5 discussed. / just / Let's / recap / we've / what
6 forward / I / look / next / speaking / to / to / week. / you

Confirmation e-mail

3 Some of the underlined phrases in the e-mail contain errors. Find and correct them.

To: Andrew Drummond
From: Kate McKay
Subject: Conference invitations

It was good to speak to you yesterday. ¹ <u>I'd just like to go</u> what we agreed.

² <u>Sum up,</u> ³ <u>you are going to deliver</u> five boxes of the conference invitations currently stored in your warehouse (code: 4543643B) to each of the three addresses below by 14 April.

⁴ <u>As agreed</u>, you will charge us a total of ☐65 – that is: two deliveries to Dublin @ ☐15 each and one delivery to Manchester @ ☐35. ⁵ <u>Are you agree?</u>

---

6 Concluding the deal

4 a Put the sentences into the correct order to reconstruct the end of a negotiation.

a   Yes, that's right. And you're going to send me the addresses.

b   Can I just summarize what we've agreed?

c   Good idea. Go ahead.

d   You're going to reprint 12,000 copies of our annual report, 10,000 of which you will mail out by 2 July, with the remainder going to our Warsaw office. Are you happy with that?

e   No problem. I look forward to speaking to you tomorrow.

f   Yes, I will – but I'll need to speak to our Marketing Department first. Can I call you tomorrow?

g   Great. Thanks for your patience. Bye.

  b 🎧 **6.4 Listen and check your answers.**

Pronunciation **5 a 🎧 6.5 Listen to an extract from the dialogue in Exercise 4. Which words are stressed? Mark the transcript on page 63.**

  b **Practise saying the phrases you heard, using the transcript.**

> **Tip** To avoid misunderstandings, stress key words (dates, times, places, people, etc.) during negotiations. Perhaps offer to spell any unusual words.

Consolidation

1 **Think of a negotiation you have recently taken part in.**
- Were you happy with the agreement made?
- Did you summarize the main points of the agreement at the end?
- Did you confirm any action points – who does what, when, etc.?
- What would you have done differently?

2 **Now think of a future negotiation you need to take part in. Note down some phrases you plan to use.**

3 **After the negotiation, take a few moments to reflect on it and complete the checklist on page 53.**

4 **Write an e-mail to the other party summarizing the agreement(s) made.**

➡ NOW TURN TO YOUR LEARNING JOURNAL AND MAKE NOTES ON THIS UNIT.

Reference

Useful phrases

Summarizing

Perhaps I could just … ?

I'd just like to …

Can I just go over / summarize (what we've agreed)?

Let's just recap / go through (what we've discussed).

To sum up/recap, …

Confirming agreement

Do you agree?

Do you have anything to add?

Have I missed anything out?

Do we need to discuss anything else?

Are you happy with that?

Please (could you) tell me if (I have missed anything out).

Responding

That's right/fine.

Agreed. / I agree.

I think that's everything/all.

I think we've/you've covered everything.

Outlining future action

So (we've agreed) you're going to / you will …

As agreed, we will / are going to …

You've agreed to …

One point we still need to agree is …

Thanking / Saying goodbye

Thank you / Thanks very much (everyone for your time).

Would you like a coffee (before you leave)?

Goodbye. I look forward to speaking to you (next week).

Vocabulary

Logistics

to agree/agreement

to confirm/confirmation

to deliver/delivery

goods

to invoice/invoice

lorry

to mail out

to order/order

to outline/outline

to pay (in full)/payment

to receive

to summarize/summary

to supply/supplier/supplies

within (five) working days

Study suggestion Note down key phrases you might need in a future negotiation. Highlight (e.g. underline) the words in each phrase that you will stress. For example: *Can I just go over your quotes for <u>storing</u> our merchandise and for <u>distributing</u> it.*

Review

Skills What four pieces of advice would you give a colleague about ending a negotiation effectively?

Useful phrases

1 🎧 **6.6** Listen to the end of a negotiation between a group of colleagues. Choose the correct option.

1 The delivery service chosen is *LMP Mail / Despatch-2-u / Go Places*.
2 *LMP Mail / Despatch-2-u / Go Places* was too expensive.
3 *LMP Mail / Despatch-2-u / Go Places* didn't offer enough services.

2 🎧 **6.6** Listen again. What phrases are used to do the following?

1 summarize
2 confirm agreement
3 outline future action
4 thank/say goodbye.

Vocabulary

1 Complete this table. Check your answers in the Reference section opposite.

Verb	Noun
1 _____	confirmation
to summarize	2 _____
3 _____	agreement
to deliver	4 _____
5 _____	outline
to pay	6 _____

2 Complete these phrases with the words in the box.

by   in   out   out   over   to   with   with

1 Have I missed anything _____ ?
2 Are you happy _____ that?
3 Can you please pay _____ the end of the month?
4 Can we go _____ what we have agreed?
5 We need to mail _____ copies this week.
6 Please could you pay _____ full.
7 As agreed, you will supply us _____ the brochures by Friday.
8 I look forward _____ speaking to you tomorrow.

Pronunciation

a Look at the transcript for audio 6.7 (page 63). Which words in each sentence would you stress?

b Practise saying the sentences.

c 🎧 **6.7** Listen and compare.

6 Concluding the deal

Resources

Note: The material on pages 46–53 may be photocopied for use in class.

Unit 1
Preparing for a negotiation (Consolidation, Exercise 1)

Preparing for a negotiation	
Consider the following	**Notes**
Your objectives (e.g. main/secondary; points you are prepared to give up/trade)	
Your approach (e.g. negotiate alone / with colleagues; the order in which to bring up your points)	
The other party (e.g. name, role, company culture; what they might want to achieve; possible objections to your proposals, compromises, shared interests)	
Language you will need (e.g. words/phrases, pronunciation)	

from *Negotiating* by Susan Lowe and Louise Pile © DELTA PUBLISHING 2007

Unit 2
Opening the negotiation (Consolidation, Exercise 1)

Opening the negotiation

Useful phrases

Welcoming/greetings and introductions

Small talk

Setting the agenda

Stating interests

Pronounciation tips

Useful vocabulary

Unit 3
Making proposals (Consolidation, Exercise 1)

Making proposals

Consider the following	Notes
Your proposals:	
Possible proposals your counterpart will make:	
Your reaction:	
Your counter-proposals:	
Diplomatic language:	
Useful vocabulary:	

Unit 4
Persuading and giving reassurance
(Practice, Exercise 4)

1 I need to know that construction work will not disturb my employees.	**2** Production cannot be disrupted. Can you guarantee to have the spare parts for the broken machine to me by the end of the week?	**3** Your company didn't supply suitable goods last month. Can you assure me that quality of the next batch will be better?	**4** Health and Safety standards have to be met. Is the lighting adequate in this office?
5 How can I reassure my staff that they will have enough desk space for the work that they do? They have heard that the new desks will be smaller than their current ones.	**6** We need meeting rooms with large screens for video-conferencing sessions. I'm not convinced this requirement went into the specification.	**7** How can I be sure you will deliver on time? You have been consistently late in the past.	**8** Your company is new on the international market. How do I know that you will give me the service I need?

Unit 4
Checking and clarifying
(Practice, Exercise 7)

Checking you've understood correctly	Showing understanding	Clarifying	I'm afraid I didn't catch what you said.
I'm sorry, did you say … ?	Yes, I see.	Right.	No, not exactly.
That's not really what I meant.	What I wanted to say was …	When you said … , did you mean … ?	OK.
I'm sorry, I didn't catch that.	A-ha, yes.	No, not … , but …	What I meant was …
I'm not sure if I've understood you correctly.	Yes, that's right.	When you say …	Well, to be more precise, …

from *Negotiating* by Susan Lowe and Louise Pile © DELTA PUBLISHING 2007

Unit 4
Reaching agreement (Consolidation, Exercise 1)

Reaching agreement

Useful phrases

Clarifying

Bargaining

Persuading

Reassuring

Pronounciation tips

Useful vocabulary

Unit 5
Checklist (Consolidation, Exercise 2)

Negotiation checklist: preparation	
Are you going to negotiate: • on your own? • as part of a team?	
What is your role in the team?	
What are other people's roles?	
What preparation do you need to do: • alone? • together?	
Who will be involved at what stage of the negotiation?	
Any phrases/vocabulary you will need	

Unit 6

Concluding a negotiation (Presentation, Exercise 3b)

Would you like	a coffee before you leave?	Do we need to	discuss anything else?
Let's just recap	what we've agreed.	So we've agreed	we will deliver tomorrow.
Are you happy	with that?	So, you're going	to send us a written summary.
I think we've	covered everything.	No, I think	that's all.

Unit 6
Checklist (Consolidation, Exercise 3)

Negotiation checklist: summary

Did you reach an agreement both parties were happy with?

Have you confirmed the terms of the agreement in writing?

Have you checked your understanding of the agreement?

Are there any points still to be agreed?

Notes:

Transcripts and answer keys

Needs analysis

Suggested answers

1 Have clear goals

   Be aware of your counterpart's goals

   Develop rapport and trust

   Explore common ground

   Be flexible and open to alternatives

   Be self-confident and persuasive

   Avoid conflict and tension

   Remain positive

   Be clear about what stage of the negotiation you are at (e.g. you are about to make a proposal)

   Give reasons for your arguments

   Summarize and test understanding

   Ask questions

   Avoid immediate responses and reactions

2/3
   Preparation
   assess and prioritize objectives; consider targets; form opinions and reasons

   Discussion
   establish rapport; small talk; state interests; show respect

   Proposals
   make offers; react to proposals; make counter-proposals, be diplomatic

   Bargaining
   check and clarify; listen between the lines; ask questions; persuade; give reassurance

   Conclusion
   summarize; confirm agreement; outline future action; say goodbye

Unit 1

Transcripts

1.1

Fiona Matrix Housing. Fiona Woodhouse speaking. How can I help?

Manolo Oh hello. This is Manolo García Puente calling from Design Express. Thank you for asking us to quote for designing your newsletter. Based on the specification you gave, that'll be £75 per page – so, £600 per issue.

F £75 a page? That sounds rather a lot ... but then I don't know much about design costs these days ...

M I assure you you'll not find a cheaper quote elsewhere – we're very professional and extremely competitive.

F Hmm ... I can't really compare, as I haven't asked anyone else for a quote – but it is more than we can afford. Um ... perhaps you'd like to reconsider your price – or offer a discount, as it's the first issue and everything.

M A discount? We don't usually offer discounts, I'm afraid.

F Well, we urgently need the newsletter designed, so we'll pay the £600 this time, but I'm afraid we won't be able to use your services in the future.

M Oh, I see. Well, I'm sorry you feel that way, but ...

1.2

▲ You know Kempsters, the large building company in Wakefield? Well, they asked us for a quote for pine flooring for the hallways in the new office block they're working on. I faxed the quote through yesterday, and their buyer, Michelle Bruce, has just called to see if we'd be prepared to lower our prices. I said I'd call her back ... I'm not sure what to say ...

✦ I see. How much would the job be worth to us?

▲ At least £25,000 for the flooring, I reckon, plus delivery, labour costs, fittings and so on.

✦ Wow! In that case, I think we should negotiate with them.

▲ I agree, but what do you think we should offer?

✦ We could drop the price by 20p per metre, <u>as that would make us cheaper than Floors4u</u>.

▲ Hmm – I don't think that's enough. Some of the bigger retailers are charging just £16.50 a metre for their stock pine flooring. I think we should reduce the cost by a pound from £16.99 to £15.99, <u>so that we're more competitive</u>.

✦ That sounds good to me. <u>I think our main aim should be to get the contract for the hallways</u>, but remember that Kempsters will need to get flooring for the office space, too. If the negotiation is going well, you could then try to get them to give us the contract for the offices, too.

▲ Good idea, but how?

✦ Perhaps offer to give them a further discount, say 5% off the total price, if they guarantee to buy all their flooring from us for the new development. <u>That way, we get a lot more business, and they save themselves money and the hassle of dealing with two suppliers.</u> Do you think their buyer would go with that?

▲ Well, Michelle is their most experienced buyer, and quite a demanding negotiator, so I've heard – she might well say 5% isn't enough and ask for 20% – I don't think we should go as high as that, <u>because it won't give us enough profits.</u>

✦ I agree. It might be better to go up to a maximum of 10%, but offer to fit the flooring for free if they demand more.

▲ Hmm – I can see your point, but if we fit it for free now, that could cause us problems in the future.

+ True ... let's offer a maximum of 10% discount if we get both contracts, but forget the free fittings. So, let me just recap on what we'll offer ... we're going to reduce the price by a pound ...

1.3

1 object / objection
2 negotiate / negotiation
3 agree / agreement
4 prepare / preparation

1.4

▲ I think we should reduce our charges so that we're more competitive.

+ I agree. We're far more expensive than other training companies. But what do you think we should charge?

▲ We could ask for $60 per hour for standard courses.

+ That's a good idea, but what do you think we should do about our specialized programs?

▲ How do you feel about charging $100? They do take longer to prepare ...

+ That sounds good to me. I'll let the rest of the team know our decisions.

1.5

1 pre<u>fer</u> 2 en<u>a</u>ble 3 ob<u>jec</u>tion 4 negoti<u>a</u>tion
5 <u>con</u>tract 6 com<u>pet</u>itive 7 main<u>tain</u>
8 <u>work</u>load 9 <u>bud</u>get 10 pro<u>po</u>sals

1.6

Karen Oh hi. Is that Pierre? Hello. This is Karen from POR Consulting. I'm calling about the quote I sent you last week for running communications skills training.

Pierre Oh yes, of course.

K I just wondered if you'd made a decision about suppliers.

P Yes, we have. I'm afraid you've been unsuccessful on this occasion.

K Oh, I see. Can you give me a reason?

P Well, your prices were at least double that of the other suppliers.

K Oh well, never mind. Um ... goodbye.

Answer key

Context

2 1 Neither has prepared very well for the negotiation. Fiona doesn't have very good knowledge about design costs, but she could have tried to find out more, e.g. getting quotes from several different suppliers, or asking colleagues for advice. Neither seems to have set their objectives. There is nothing to be gained from making a deal at all costs – Fiona could have turned down the quote and gone to someone else less expensive.

2 The negotiation is not very successful. The supplier is not thinking flexibly or long term – he could have given a discount for the first issue and agreed a price to design the next two/three/four, etc. issues of the magazine. Fiona could have helped him see the long-term view – it's the first issue and the first negotiation they are having, but agreeing a price they are both happy with for a number of years or issues would save Fiona having to negotiate a new deal with a new supplier each time – and the supplier would have valuable long-term business.
Both have missed opportunities by not fully understanding each other's needs or being open-minded enough.

Presentation

1 1 (pine) flooring   2 Michelle Bruce, senior buyer from Kempsters   3 to get their business providing flooring for hallways   4 to get the business for providing flooring for offices too   5 dropping their price by 20p/£1 per metre; giving 5%/10% off the total price if Kempsters buy all the flooring from them; free fitting   6 Michelle might ask for 20% off   7 drop price to £15.99 per metre and offer a maximum of 10% discount

2 I think we should ... , I agree, What do you think ... ?, We could ... , I don't think ... , I think we should ... , That sounds good to me, I think ... , Good idea, Do you think ... ?, I don't think we should ... , I agree, It might be ... , I can see your point

3 1 I think our main aim should be to get the contract for the hallways
2 as that would make us cheaper than Floors4u, so that we are more competitive, That way, we get a lot more business, and they save themselves money and the hassle of dealing with two suppliers, because it won't give us enough profits.

4 1 ob<u>ject</u> / ob<u>jec</u>tion   3 a<u>gree</u> / a<u>gree</u>ment
2 neg<u>o</u>tiate / negoti<u>a</u>tion   4 pre<u>pare</u> / prepar<u>a</u>tion

Practice

1 1 c 2 f 3 a 4 b 5 e 6 d
2 c, d, a, b, f, e
3 1 prefer; enable   2 as; because   3 so that
4 main; as   5 That way
4 See transcript.

Review

Skills

2 Karen could have prepared her phone call more effectively, by deciding what to say if Pierre rejected their quote based on price. She could have worked out realistic discounts to offer, or have tried to negotiate on quality rather than just price, e.g. by stressing the experience of her trainers, the luxurious facilities. She could have also found out more about the rates other organizations were offering, so as to be as competitive as possible.

Useful phrases

1 I don't think we should ~~to~~ sign the contract.
2 How do you feel about **negotiating** on your own?
3 correct
4 What **are your thoughts** on lowering the price?
5 correct
6 Our main aim ought **to** be agreeing a realistic schedule.

Vocabulary

1 specification   2 to quote   3 agreement   4 to fit
5 charge(s)   6 to negotiate

Pronunciation

to a<u>gree</u>/<u>agree</u>ment
to <u>aim</u>/<u>aim</u>
to <u>budget</u>/<u>budget</u>
to <u>charge</u>/<u>charges</u>
compe<u>ti</u>tive
<u>dis</u>count
<u>fee</u>
to <u>fit</u>/<u>fittings</u>
<u>issue</u>
to ne<u>go</u>tiate/nego<u>ti</u>ation/ne<u>go</u>tiator
to <u>lower</u> (a price)
ob<u>jec</u>tive
to pre<u>pare</u>/prepar<u>a</u>tion
to <u>quote</u>/<u>quote</u>
to re<u>duce</u> (a price)
satis<u>fac</u>tory
specifi<u>ca</u>tion
to suc<u>ceed</u>/suc<u>cess</u>

Unit 2

Transcripts

2.1

Martin Stewart Good morning, ladies and gentlemen, welcome to Leclerc Electronics. My name is Martin Stewart, and these are my colleagues Valérie Dupont and Hubert Chevalier.

Emma Sadera Good morning and thank you. We're happy to be here. I'm Emma Sadera, Head of Sales at By Design. This is my assistant, Simon Clark.

MS Pleased to meet you. I hope you had a good journey.

ES Yes, the flight was fine, and just a slight delay on the roads because of heavy traffic.

MS Have you been to Lyon before, Mr Clark?

Simon Clark No, this is my first visit, so I'm looking forward to seeing some of the sights – if our schedule allows it, of course. Oh, and call me Simon, please.

Valérie Dupont Ah, you must make time to visit some of our restaurants – Lyon is famous for its cuisine, you know.

MS Right, shall we get down to business? I suggest we start by clarifying what is needed, and then we'll see whether we can do business together. OK?

ES Fine.

MS Well, I'm sure you're aware from our telephone conversation and email exchange that Leclerc Electronics is looking to expand into new markets. We have a solid client base in France, Belgium, Spain and Luxembourg, but we're hoping to open up in the rest of Europe and possibly into the USA. An important consideration for us is to portray the correct image – a good-quality electronics firm with modern ideas and up-to-date products. We want a new image that will be recognized internationally.

ES Right, By Design is keen to work with well-known companies like Leclerc Electronics, but we aim only to accept contracts where we can be sure of providing a top-quality service, which means we need to have a detailed brief and one contact person who remains the same throughout the project.

MS That sounds reasonable. We should be able to assign …

2.2

1 Welcome to Sanicare Installations.
2 I'd like to welcome you all this morning.
3 Are you looking forward to seeing the Eiffel Tower?
4 Our company is keen to work with upcoming companies.
5 We need to decide the schedules by the end of the week.
6 He's hoping to sign the contract as soon as possible.

2.3

1 ▲ Perhaps we don't need to discuss that now.
   + No, I'm afraid we need to.
2 ▲ I'm not sure if you'd like to see some of the sights while you are here.
   + Yes, I'd like to.
3 ▲ Monsieur Rivot hasn't really got time to get involved in this project.
   + That's a shame, as he's very keen to.

2.4

1 Welcome to Brightside Datasystems.
2 May I introduce myself, my name is Sarah Beecham.
3 This is my secretary, Tim Hunt.
4 Did you have a good journey?
5 Unfortunately, there was a problem with the flight – we had to wait for two hours!
6 This is your first visit to Dubai, I believe.
7 I'm looking forward to seeing some of the sights.

Answer key

Context
1 1 b 2 e 3 a 4 d 5 c

3 Different cultures react in different ways. Some cultures spend more time on small talk than other cultures, and some prefer to get down to business more quickly. Setting and following a strict agenda is important to some cultures, whereas others prefer to be more flexible.

Presentation
1 1 False 2 False 3 False 4 True 5 False 6 True

2 1 g 2 i 3 k 4 b 5 e 6 d 7 h 8 f 9 a 10 j 11 c

3 Additional phrases are shown in italics.

Welcoming	1
Introducing yourself/ colleagues	2 *These are my colleagues, Valérie Dupont and Hubert Chevalier. This is my assistant, Simon Clark.*
Small talk	3, 4 *I'm looking forward to seeing some of the sights.*
Setting the agenda	5, 6
Stating interests	7, 8, 9, 10, 11 *We have a solid client base in France. We aim to only accept contracts where we can be sure of providing a top-quality service.*

4 1 d 2 e 3 b 4 f 5 a 6 c 7 g

5
a The pronunciation of the *o* in each *to* is short because the word/sound is followed by another word which takes the stress.

b The pronunciation of the *o* in each *to* is long because the word *to* is the final word of the sentence and therefore carries the stress.

Practice
1 a 1 to 2 myself 3 This 4 have 5 delay/problem 6 visit/trip; believe/understand/think 7 forward; seeing/visiting

b Note that only one version each of sentences 5, 6 and 7 has been recorded (the most natural-sounding version).

2
1 Shall we get down to business?
2 I suggest we start by clarifying the situation.
3 We are looking to expand into new markets.
4 An important consideration for us is to keep existing customers.
5 We aim to develop business in the USA.
6 We are keen to maintain high quality.

3
1 We **have** a good reputation.
2 Our clients **need** to give us a detailed brief.
3 Maynard Plc **is** currently **looking** to promote sales in Europe.
4 Our Head of Marketing **is launching** a new campaign this month.
5 **Does** your Director **want** a decision today?
6 **Are** you **looking** forward to visiting our city while you are here this week?

4 *Suggested answers*
1 This is my colleague, Élodie Hussain.
2 Is your hotel is comfortable?
3 Let's begin by outlining the current situation.
4 We aim to launch our advertising campaign before the summer.
5 We hope to see a rise in sales by the end of the year.

Review
Useful phrases
1 See Reference section
2 1 hope 2 have 3 is holding 4 Are you visiting

Vocabulary

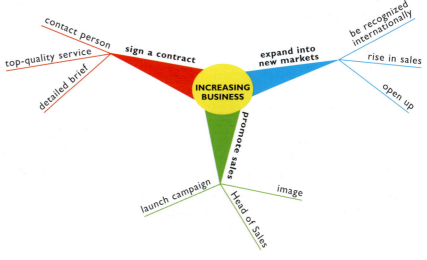

Unit 3

Transcripts

3.1

Boss Morning, John, Paul … How are you both?

John Fine, thanks.

Paul Fine.

B Hello, Helga, come in. Have you seen Thomas? Ah, here he is.

Thomas Hello.

B OK, thanks everyone for sparing some time today for this meeting – I know you're all busy. I wanted to get you all together to discuss your workload. Since Regina left, it's been difficult, I know. The Human Resources Department have advertised the vacancy, but it could take a couple of months to have someone in place. So, in the meantime, I'd like to propose that John moves from his current project and works with Thomas. Helga, I suggest that you stay where you are – Paul can help out if need be, as he knows that client. Paul, I'd like you to take on the new contract that's just come in.

Helga That sounds OK to me.

J I'm afraid I have some reservations about moving from my project. I know it's nearly finished, but I propose that I see it through to the end. Could Thomas work on his own for a while instead?

B Hm, I understand your concern, but the project Thomas is working on is worth $250,000, whereas yours is only $30,000, so I'm afraid it's not really possible to have just one person on that project. Perhaps a better idea would be for Paul to work with Thomas and you, John, take on the new contract just in.

P That sounds reasonable.

J Yes, I can agree to that.

B Everyone else?

H/T Fine.

B Good, so that's settled, then. If you've got any specific concerns …

3.2

1 I propose that you stay in this team.
2 We suggest postponing the project.
3 I can't agree to that, I'm afraid.
4 Could we delay the start date instead?
5 Yes, we can accept those conditions.

3.3

1 My proposal is that Owen takes over as project leader.
2 We'd like to propose reorganizing the team.
3 Our proposal is to outsource management of the next project.
4 I suggest that Sue and Matthew work together on the design for this project.

3.4

1 We suggest starting again.
2 I propose forming a new team.
3 We suggest asking our customers what they want.
4 I propose that we do some research first.
5 I'm afraid that's not really acceptable.
6 How about using a new supplier?
7 That's a good idea!

Answer key

Context

1 1 a counter-proposal   2 diplomatic language

2 The answer will depend on you, but many people find responding to proposals more difficult because you need time to digest what has been offered and react appropriately.

Presentation

1 a Grouping B
   b Grouping A

2 1 I'd like to propose that   2 I suggest that
   3 That sounds OK   4 I'm afraid I have some reservations about   5 Could   6 I understand your concern   7 I'm afraid it's not really possible   8 Perhaps a better idea would be   9 That sounds reasonable   10 Yes, I can agree to that   11 Fine

3 1 Accepting proposals   2 Rejecting proposals
   3 Making counter-proposals   4 Making proposals

4 1 I'm afraid I have some reservations about moving from my project.
   2 I understand your concern.
   3 I'm afraid it's not really possible to have just one person on that project.

5 1 c   2 a   3 d   4 b

6 1 we stay   2 suggest that   3 propose   4 moving

7 1 a   2 d   3 b   4 e   5 c

Practice

1 *Suggested answers*

   1 That sounds like a good idea. Owen has lots of experience.
   2 I'm afraid that's unacceptable. It would cause too much disruption.
   3 I can't agree to that, I'm afraid, as it didn't work last time. Could we promote one of the team members as a development opportunity instead?
   4 Yes, I can agree to that. They work well together.

2 *Suggested answers*

   1 I'd like to propose that we share the workload more equally.
   2 My colleagues and I suggest holding an update meeting each week.
   3 We propose delaying the start date by one month.
   4 Having considered your proposals, my boss suggests we accept your offer.

5 Last time we met, we proposed that you reworked your brief so we were clearer what you expected of us.

3 *Suggested answers*
 1 That's not really possible, I'm afraid.
 2 I'm sorry, but that's not really acceptable.
 3 We can't accept that, I'm afraid.
 4 That's rather more than we wanted to spend.
 5 We would appreciate quicker delivery.

4 a 1 We <u>suggest</u> <u>start</u>ing a<u>gain</u>.
   2 I pro<u>pose</u> <u>form</u>ing a new <u>team</u>.
   3 We <u>suggest</u> <u>ask</u>ing our <u>cust</u>omers <u>what</u> they <u>want</u>.
   4 I pro<u>pose</u> that we <u>do</u> some res<u>earch</u> first.
   5 I'm a<u>fraid</u> that's <u>not</u> <u>real</u>ly ac<u>cep</u>table.
   6 <u>How</u> about <u>us</u>ing a <u>new</u> sup<u>pli</u>er?
   7 <u>That's</u> a good i<u>dea</u>!

Review

Skills
1 reject 2 counter-proposal 3 diplomatic
4 accept

Useful phrases
1 See Reference section on page 24.
2 1 outsourcing 2 delaying 3 changing
  4 reorganizing

Vocabulary
1 to postpone a project 2 project leader
3 to see a project through 4 to reorganize the team
5 to propose / to make a proposal
6 to make a counter-proposal

Unit 4

Transcripts

4.1

So, in the bargaining phase of a negotiation, when you put conditions to the offers you are making, your business partner won't necessarily accept immediately. This is because he or she is probably starting with a different viewpoint to you, and a first step in avoiding argument is to show respect for your partner's opinion and needs. Never say 'you are wrong'. Instead, try to see things from your partner's point of view. When trying to persuade your partner, make them feel important, show respect, and let your partner feel the solution is their idea. Let them do the talking. You need to be a good listener. Check and clarify a few issues to prove that you really are listening, and it helps you to 'read between the lines' to establish what they really are saying. If your partner remains unsure, give them reassurance, talk in terms of their interests and demonstrate how agreement can benefit you both.

4.2

Terry Norton I'm not sure if I've understood you correctly. Am I right in thinking that you need some rooms to be used as quiet rooms in addition to normal meeting rooms?

Tita Aiguillar Yes, that's right. I can assure you that the number of rooms required is no different to the agreed plans, we just need to have them assigned slightly differently. If you put in phone lines and Internet access to all the rooms, we could use any as a meeting room or a quiet room and it won't make any difference to your plans.

TN When you say you can use any room, what do you mean exactly?

TA I mean we could use the room for a meeting – perhaps for a teleconference – or equally, a member of staff may need to phone a colleague abroad, which will take a long time, so they could use the telephone in the room instead of at their desk, to avoid disturbing their colleagues.

TN I see.

TA The other issue we need to clarify is how much storage my staff will have. If you can provide extra storage somewhere on the floor for the archive my members of staff need access to, then we are prepared to manage with a small cupboard behind each desk.

TN Would it be correct to say your staff don't need access to the archives very often?

TA No, that's not really accurate. I would say almost on a daily basis.

TN Hm. I'm sure you're aware we have limited space, and what we have needs to be divided between your department and the marketing department. You can be sure that your department has the standard amount of storage and that it will be located as near as possible to your staff.

4.3

Tita Aiguillar The other issue we need to clarify is how much storage my staff will have. If you can provide extra storage somewhere on the floor for the archive my members of staff need access to, then we are prepared to manage with a small cupboard behind each desk.

Terry Norton Would it be correct to say your staff don't need access to the archives very often?

TA No, that's not really accurate. I would say almost on a daily basis.

TN Hm. I'm sure you're aware we have limited space, and what we have needs to be divided between your department and the Marketing Department. You can be sure that your department has the standard amount of storage and that it will be located as near as possible to your staff.

4.4

I mean we could use the room for a meeting – perhaps for a teleconference – or equally, a member of staff may need to phone a colleague abroad, which will take a long time, so they could use the telephone in the room instead of at their desk, to avoid disturbing their colleagues.

4.5

1 I understand your concerns about noise and dirt. You can be sure that the strictest health and safety regulations have been followed.

2 I appreciate the fact that you don't want the construction work to cause delays for your research. I can assure you that we will do our very best to avoid that.

3 I realize that you are worried about storage space. I assure you that we will provide you with the standard amount.

4.6

1 I'm not sure if I've understood you correctly.

2 Would it be correct to say that you don't need teleconferencing facilities in all the meeting rooms?

3 Provided you can guarantee high-quality goods, I'll accept your offer.

4.7

1 Our deadline is the thirteenth of May.

2 We can't make that decision right now. We'll have to report back to our Head of Unit, who in turn will feed back to the Committee. If they're satisfied that the outcome will be beneficial to our members, then we could accept your offer.

3 I think you said you could offer a 10% discount if we paid by the end of the month. Is that right?

4 So [you've heard both proposals], what do you think?

5 So we need you to guarantee quick delivery.

6 I believe you agreed to sign the contract by the end of the week.

Answer key

Context

Persuading: make partner feel important, show respect, let them feel solution is their idea.

Listening: Let them do the talking, be a good listener

Checking and clarifying: check and clarify to prove you are listening, to read between the lines

Giving reassurance: talk in terms of their interests, show how agreement can be of benefit to both parties

Presentation

1 1, 4

2 1 phone lines and Internet access
   2 avoid disturbing colleagues
   3 the archive
   4 almost every day

3 1 can guarantee that; accept the proposal
   2 Provided that; then we could   3 If you; we could
   4 If you can; we are prepared   5 you'll agree that
   6 you'll appreciate that   7 assure you that
   8 can be sure that

4 1 c   2 d   3 e   4 b   5 a

5 1 False   2 False

6 I mean we could use the room for a meeting, perhaps for a teleconference, or equally, a member of staff may need to phone a colleague abroad which will take a long time, so they could use the telephone in the room instead of at their desk, to avoid disturbing their colleagues.

7 I'm not sure if I've understood you correctly.
Am I right in thinking that … ?
Yes, that's right.
When you say … , what do you mean exactly?
I mean …
Would it be correct to say … ?
No, that's not really accurate.

Practice

1 b, a, d, f, c, e, g

2 1 If you can guarantee that
   2 then we will accept the proposal   3 Provided
   4 we could   5 If you   6 can

3 1 moved   2 shared   3 can start   4 will become
   5 would use   6 continue

4 *Suggested answers*

1 I can assure you that the construction work will not disturb your employees.

2 I'm sure you will appreciate that we will do our best regarding delivery.

3 I know you'll agree that generally quality has been adequate.

4 You can be sure that Health and Safety standards have been adhered to.

5 You can be sure that all desks meet the specified requirements.

6 I can assure you that the screens will be in place.

7 I'm sure you understand that we occasionally have a problem with our distributors. This has now been resolved.

8 I know you'll agree that the service you have received so far has been excellent.

5 1 b   2 b   3 b

6 1 I'm not sure if I've understood you correctly.

2 Would it be correct to say that you don't need teleconferencing facilities in all meeting rooms?

3 Provided you can guarantee high-quality goods, I'll accept your offer.

7   a **Checking you've understood correctly**

   I'm sorry, did you say … ?

   I'm sorry, I didn't catch that.

   I'm not sure if I've understood you correctly.

   When you said … , did you mean … ?

   When you say …

   I'm afraid I didn't catch what you said.

   Showing understanding

   Yes, I see. / Right. / OK.

   A-ha, yes.

   Clarifying

   No, not exactly.

   That's not really what I meant.

   What I wanted to say was …

   No, not … , but …

   What I meant was …

   Yes, that's right.

   Well, to be more precise …

   c *Suggested answers*

   1 Did you say the thirteenth?

   2 I'm not sure if I've understood you correctly. Do you mean I'll have to wait for a decision?

   3 Yes, that's right.

   4 I'm afraid I didn't catch what you said.

   5 When you say quick delivery, how soon do you need it?

   6 No, not exactly. I meant I would let you know by the end of the week whether we accept your offer.

Review

Skills

See answers for Context on page 60.

Useful phrases

1   1 I'm not sure if I've understood you correctly.

   2 Provided disturbance is minimal, we agree to the work starting next month.

   3 I know you'll agree that …

   4 I can assure you that …

2   1 will order   2 would be delayed
   3 would be installed   4 will drop

Vocabulary

Across 1 plans   2 storage   5 room   6 disturb

Down   1 Provided   3 access   4 floor

> **Grammar note**
>
> To form the first conditional, use *if* + *(do)* + *will/can/may (do)*.
> If you **reduce** the price, **I'll accept** your offer.
>
> To form the second conditional, use *if* + *(did)* + *would/could/might (do)*:
> If you **reduced** the price, **I'd accept** your offer.

Unit 5

Transcripts

5.1

Peter Good morning, everyone! I hope you've all had a good weekend. We're all here in the Frankfurt office – Hans …

Hans Morning!

P … Esther …

Esther Hi!

P … and me, of course – Peter! What about London, Anna?

Anna I'm afraid Sam's off sick, so it's just me and Mark.

Mark Hello.

P Right, let's get started, shall we? Esther, would you mind taking notes?

E Mm, that's fine.

P Thanks. As I'm sure you all know, the communications team has been asked to put together the company's annual report again this year, and we need to decide who's going to do what. Anna, would your team be able to manage things this year, as we took the lead last year?

A Hmm. How much time will it take, do you think?

P About a week's work – spread over a couple of months.

A Hmm, Mark, what do you think?

M Hmm. We are quite busy here. What's the deadline?

P We've got until the 23rd of March to get it produced and printed copies made.

M I see. Could you tell us exactly what it would involve?

P Perhaps you could answer that, Hans? You did most of the work on it last year.

H Well, you need to get various staff members to write about the work that's taken place in their departments, plus an introduction by the CEO, and then financial reports from the Finance Department …

M Just a minute while I note that down.

H You don't need to. I'll draw you up a list of who I contacted last year if you like.

A/M Oh, yes, thanks. / Thank you.

A Who needs to sign off the report?

P The senior management team will need to see and check the final version. Ah, Geoff from Marketing has just come into the office. I'll just ask him what's going to happen … So, OK, he's confirmed it needs to go to the CEO as well as the senior management team.

A Well, OK, we'll take it on, but only if your team, Peter, agrees to help out if we're too busy.

P/H/E Of course. / Yes, OK.

P Would you like to ask anything else at this stage? Anna? Mark?

M Hans, could you say something about the editing and design stages, please?
H You'll need to get the document into …

5.2
1 What's the deadline?
2 Could you tell us exactly what that would involve?
3 Who needs to sign off the report?

5.3
1
▲ What is the deadline for getting the delivery to you?
✚ Around the middle of next week, I'd say.
2
▲ So, why should I place an order with you and not another stationery company?
✚ Brian, perhaps you'd like to answer that?
3
▲ Why are you just offering us 10 per cent off? As a valued customer we expect a lot more than that.
✚ That's a good point. I'll speak to Sanjit and get back to you.
4
▲ Could you tell me when you'll be making a decision?
✚ I'd like to talk about that in just a minute.

Answer key

Context
Suggested answers
2 Working in a team can be very effective, particularly where members of the team have different skills or knowledge, such as financial expertise. It's also useful to have people who can take on different roles in the negotiation, for example, note-taker or leader. However, preparation can be more time-consuming, as you will need to make sure that everyone knows their role and has the same objectives. It can happen that people contradict each other.
3 All members are prepared for the negotiations and have the same objectives, know who should be involved when in the negotiation, etc.
4 A negotiation may not just be a one-off event, but a series of meetings, phone calls, e-mails and so on, and you might need to involve others in any stage of the negotiating process, from the planning stage to making a deal. For example:
   • You might spend months persuading another company to agree to work together on a joint project, but perhaps more senior staff would then need to be involved in a further negotiation – to sign the contract, agree the roles each party would take, etc.
   • You may feel confident negotiating the price of delivering a consignment, for example, but before making a deal, you decide to call a colleague from production to confirm the deadlines or agree schedules.
   • You might decide to use a mediator when a negotiation breaks down.
   • In areas outside your expertise you may feel you aren't the best person to conduct the negotiation at all and you employ someone else to negotiate for you, for instance, when buying a house. In this case, you will need to brief the negotiator well and monitor discussions closely.

Presentation
1 1 F (there are five)   2 F (Peter)   3 T
2 1, 3, 5, 8, 10
3 a 1 c   2 b   3 d   4 a
   b 1 What's the deadline?
      2 Could you tell us exactly what that would involve?
      3 Who needs to sign off the report?
5 I'll draw you up a list … ; I'll just ask him … ; we'll take it on …
6 1 Just a minute while I note that down.
   2 Please bear with me while I find out what's happened.
   3 Excuse me while I send a quick e-mail.

Practice
1 1 Perhaps you could ~~to~~ answer that question, Sandra?
   2 **Let's** ask Alexis about the plans.
   3 *correct*
   4 Could you **say** something about the planning stage, Siobhan?
   5 I'm sure you'll all ~~be~~ agree that it's a good idea.
   6 Please bear **with** me while I make a quick phone call.
   7 Just a minute **while** I consult a colleague.
   8 Would you like **to** ask anything else?
3 *Suggested answers*
   1 I'll give you a hand.
   2 Sure, I'll give you a lift.
   3 I know – I'm going to ask Stefan for some help right now.
   4 Actually, I feel awful and am going to go home.

Review
Vocabulary
1 b   2 d   3 a   4 f   5 e   6 c

Unit 6

Transcripts

6.1

Emily So, can I just go over what we've agreed? You're going to supply us with 100 bottles of still and 200 bottles of sparkling water, to be delivered directly to the Hotel Splendido in Milan on the 15th of March. The total cost to us will be €456, which we have agreed to pay in full within 25 working days of receiving the delivery. Have I missed anything out?

Supplier No, I think that's all, Emily … oh, one final point we need to agree, I think, is a suitable delivery time.

E Oh, yes, as I said before, the earlier the better! Shall we speak on the phone next week?

S Good idea, Emily. I'll ring you on Thursday.

E OK. I look forward to speaking to you again then. By the way, good luck with your tennis match on Saturday!

S Oh, thanks. I'd almost forgotten about that. Goodbye!

6.2

1 You're going to supply us with <u>100</u> bottles of <u>still</u> and <u>200</u> bottles of <u>sparkling</u> water.
2 The total cost to us will be <u>€456</u>.
3 We have agreed to pay in full within <u>25 working days</u>.

6.3

1 ▲ Are you happy with that?
   + Yes, that's fine.
2 ▲ Do we need to discuss anything else?
   + No, I think we've covered everything.
3 ▲ Do you have anything to add?
   + No, I think that's all.
4 ▲ Do you agree?
   + Yes, agreed.
5 ▲ Have I missed anything out?
   + No, that's right.

6.4

▲ Can I just summarize what we've agreed?
+ Good idea. Go ahead.
▲ You're going to reprint 12,000 copies of our annual report, 10,000 of which you will mail out by the 2nd of July, with the remainder going to our Warsaw office. Are you happy with that?
+ Yes, that's right. And you're going to send me the addresses.
▲ Yes, I will – but I'll need to speak to our Marketing Department first. Can I call you tomorrow?
+ No problem. I look forward to speaking to you tomorrow.
▲ Great. Thanks for your patience. Bye.

6.5

You're going to reprint 12,000 copies of our annual report, 10,000 of which you will mail out by the 2nd of July, with the remainder going to our Warsaw office. Are you happy with that?

6.6

▲ Right, I think we've finally decided on a delivery service for our company to use in future. So, let's recap what we've agreed. Out of the three delivery companies that were suggested, we've decided against LMP Mail as they are too dear. Despatch-2-u don't offer a same-day delivery service, which we need, so they're out. So, we've agreed to use Go Places, which offers the range of services we require at reasonable rates. Do you have anything to add? Teresa?
+ No, I agree.
▲ Lucas?
● No, I think you've covered everything.
▲ Good, so, as agreed, Lucas, you'll contact the delivery companies concerned and tell them our decision. I'll e-mail the rest of the team and let them know. If that's all, thank you all for your time.

6.7

1 I didn't say 13 boxes, I said 30.
2 Could you deliver to the Hotel Martinique, not the Hotel Martin?
3 I'd like Lucy to sort out the delivery arrangements – rather than Ian.
4 Please deliver the goods by Friday at the latest.
5 The lorry needs to go to Litzelstetten. Shall I spell that for you?
6 As agreed, you'll deliver by 4 p.m.
7 I'll send your order confirmation through tomorrow.

Answer key

Presentation

1 1 F   2 T   3 F   4 T

2 1 b   2 b   3 a   4 a

3 Phrases from the cards are shown in italics.

Summarizing	Confirming agreement / Responding	Outlining future action	Thanking / Saying goodbye
Perhaps I could just summarize what we've agreed? Can I just go over what we've agreed? *Let's just recap what we've agreed.*	Do you have anything to add? Have I missed anything out? Do we need to discuss anything else? Are you happy with that? I think we've covered everything. *No, I think that's all.*	One point we need to agree is a suitable delivery time. As agreed, we will contact you about a suitable delivery time. *So we've agreed we will deliver tomorrow.* *So you're going to send us a written summary.*	I look forward to speaking to you again then. Bye. Thank you – and goodbye. *Would you like a coffee before you leave?*

4 See transcript.

Practice

1 1 e   2 c   3 b   4 a   5 d

2 1 Perhaps I could just summarize what we've agreed.
2 Thank you for everything.
3 Do we need to discuss anything else?
4 As agreed, we will send you a written summary.
5 Let's just recap what we've discussed.
6 I look forward to speaking to you next week.

3 1 I'd just like to go **over**   2 **To** sum up   3 *correct*
4 *correct*   5 **Do** you agree?

4 b, c, d, a, f, e, g

5 You're going to reprint **12,000** copies of our annual report, **10,000** of which you will mail out by **2 July**, with the remainder going to our **Warsaw** office. Are you happy with that?

Review

Useful phrases

1 1 Go Places   2 LMP Mail   3 Despatch-2-u

2 1 So, let's recap what we've agreed; So, we've agreed to use Go Places …
2 Do you have anything to add?; No, I agree; No, I think you've covered everything.
3 So, as agreed, Lucas, you'll contact … ; I'll e-mail the rest of the team …
4 Thank you all for your time.

Vocabulary

1 1 to confirm   2 summary   3 to agree   4 delivery
5 to outline   6 payment

2 1 out   2 with   3 by   4 over   5 out   6 in
7 with   8 to

Pronunciation

1 I didn't say 13 boxes, I said 30.

2 Could you deliver to the Hotel Martinique, not the Hotel Martin?

3 I'd like Lucy to sort out the delivery arrangements – rather than Ian.

4 Please deliver the goods by Friday at the latest.

5 The lorry needs to go to Litzelstetten. Shall I spell that for you?

6 As agreed, you'll deliver by 4 p.m.

7 I'll send your order confirmation through tomorrow.